The Christmas Story

Published by Standard Publishing, Cincinnati, Ohio
www.standardpub.com.

ISBN 978-0-7847-2058-5

15 14 13 12 11 10 4 5 6 7 8 9 10 11 12

Cincinnati, Ohio

The angel said to Mary, "You will give birth to a son. . . . He will be called the Son of God." *Luke 1:31, 35*

Mary went to stay with her cousin Elizabeth for three months.

The angel visited Joseph in a dream and said,
"You will name the son Jesus." *Matthew 1:21*

Mary and Joseph had to travel to Bethlehem to be counted.

There was no room for them in the inn.

The innkeeper offered his warm stable to Mary and Joseph.

That night, Mary gave birth to Jesus in the stable.

Mary wrapped the baby with cloths and laid him in a manger.

An angel appeared to shepherds who were watching their sheep in the nearby fields.

The angel said to them, "Today your Savior was born in David's town. He is Christ, the Lord." *Luke 2:11*

When the angel left, the shepherds ran to find baby Jesus in the stable.

Mary was amazed when she heard what the angel had said about her child.

Some wise men from the east saw a special star in the sky.

The wise men followed the star until it stopped above the place where Jesus was.

The wise men brought treasures of gold, frankincense, and myrrh to honor the baby king.